BASEBALL

THE PERFECT GAME

PHOTOGRAPHS BY DANIELLE WEIL
INTRODUCTION BY DAVID HALBERSTAM
TEXT BY PETER RICHMOND

RIZZOLI
NEW YORK

THIS BOOK IS DEDICATED WITH LOVE AND SPECIAL THANKS TO MY FATHER, KURT WEIL, AND TO DAVID BURR

ACKNOWLEDGMENTS:

TO ROBERT BROWN, NANCY DROSD, NATHANIEL LANDY, BARBARA MARCUS,
CYNTHIA O'NEAL, VIVIAN POLAK, SUSAN AND JOHN ROTHCHILD,
JERRY SCHATZBERG, GEORGE STEINBRENNER, AND PAUL SYLBERT
FOR THEIR VARIOUS CONTRIBUTIONS AND GENEROUS SUPPORT

TO JANE COWEN, CHARLES DAVEY, CHARLES MIERS,
STEVEN SCHOENFELDER, PAUL WHEELER, AND PAUL WILLIAMS
FOR HELPING TO MAKE THIS BOOK A REALITY

TO CHUCK ADAMS, BRIAN BARTOW, DICK BRESCIANI, NED COLLETTI,
DAN EWALD, JAY HORWITZ, JEFF IDELSON, DICK KRAFT,
JIM LACHIMIA, LARRY SHENK, HOWARD STARKMAN,
AND RICK VAUGHN FOR MAKING BASEBALL ACCESSIBLE TO ME

TO CHELLY, SABRINA, LIZE, TAYLOR, AND PHILLIP FOR THEIR
LOVE, PATIENCE, AND ENCOURAGEMENT
– D.W.

FIRST PUBLISHED IN THE UNITED STATES OF AMERICA IN 1992
BY RIZZOLI INTERNATIONAL PUBLICATIONS, INC.
300 PARK AVENUE SOUTH, NEW YORK, NY 10010

PRINTED IN JAPAN
DESIGNED BY STEVEN SCHOENFELDER

LIBRARY OF CONGRESS CATALOGING–IN–PUBLICATION DATA
RICHMOND, PETER
BASEBALL: THE PERFECT GAME/INTRODUCTION BY DAVID HALBERSTAM;
PHOTOGRAPHS BY DANIELLE WEIL; TEXT BY PETER RICHMOND.
P.   CM.
ISBN 0-8478-1524-2 (HC) 0-8478-1493-9 (PBK)
1. BASEBALL–UNITED STATES.   2. BASEBALL–UNITED STATES–PICTORIAL WORKS.   I. WEIL, DANIELLE.   II. TITLE
GV863.A1R524 1992
796.357 0974—DC20   91-34778
CIP

COVER IMAGE:
KANSAS CITY ROYALS VS. NEW YORK YANKEES. YANKEE STADIUM. JULY 1990.

THE KANSAS CITY ROYALS AND NEW YORK YANKEES UNIFORM MARKS DEPICTED ON THE COVER
WERE REPRODUCED WITH THE PERMISSION OF MAJOR LEAGUE BASEBALL PROPERTIES, INC.

CONTENTS

INTRODUCTION BY DAVID HALBERSTAM

–5–

SPRING TRAINING

–13–

THE STADIUM

–27–

PREGAME WARM-UPS

–49–

THE GAME

–69–

THE EQUIPMENT

–115–

INTRODUCTION
DAVID HALBERSTAM

It is the early fall of 1941. I am with my father, who is a doctor in the Bronx, and he is taking me with him on his rounds this day. The radio in the car is on and it is the World Series, though the gravity of the occasion that holds the rest of the city in its hand—a ''subway series,'' as it was then known; the Yankees are playing the Dodgers—has not yet dawned on me. I am only seven. I am not excited about the Yankees being in the World Series, as most young fans would be; I have already come to assume that they will win the pennant. My father and I are Yankee fans by dint of geography; at the time we live only about seven blocks from the Stadium. I am not yet a particularly knowledgeable fan. That will come later. I know in the most simple way befitting a little boy that the Yankees are the good team and they are supposed to win if it is a just world, that the Dodgers are the bad team, and that the Yankees have my heroes, DiMaggio, Henrich, and Keller, on their team.

Two years earlier my father had taken me to Yankee Stadium, so in some small elemental way as we ride in his car and listen to the radio I can visualize the astonishing green of the grass and the majestic quality of the Yankees, who seem so immense to a boy. My father is not pleased with the way this game is going—the Yankees are losing—and he is on edge. He smokes heavily anyway, and at moments like this he chain-smokes. We are driving under the elevated; it is late in the game. The static caused by the elevated lines becomes heavier and tends to obliterate much of the sound of what I now suspect was Mel Allen's voice. There are two out, it is the ninth inning, and Tommy Henrich is up (some of this I will be able to piece together only later). My father pulls the car over to a side street so that the broadcast will not be impeded. The static is reduced. Someone named Casey is pitching. There are two strikes on Henrich. He strikes out. I hear my father curse. Then there is a great deal of shouting over the radio, more noise than clarity. My father tries to explain what has happened: the catcher Mickey Owen has dropped the ball, Henrich has reached first (a play that defies the comprehension of a seven year old). The Yankees respond to this rarest of offerings by following with a barrage of hits. My father sits in the car with me, trying to explain. The Dodgers are finished, he says, the series is over. No team can come back from something as devastating as this. In addition the Yankees now have a 3–1 edge in games. Years after I am sitting with Henrich in a small town in Arizona and he is replaying the game for me, the exact moment of Casey's pitch (others claimed later that Casey threw a spitter but both Henrich and Owen agree that Casey simply reached back and put too much on his curve and the ball broke too much).

I write this fifty years later. Those events of the 1941 World Series are far distant yet still clear in my memory. Sounds and smells to a little boy sharing something with his father. The smell of my father's cigarettes. The shadow cast by the elevated train. The static on the radio and then the din as the crowd obliterates the announcer merge that scene in my mind with other events from the fall of 1941. They all blend together: the Yankees have won the World Series, my first—that is, the first I can remember; there is more talk of war in our home, and even though America is not yet at war, we talk of it more and more in our home because events in Europe do not seem so distant to those in a Jewish American home. My uncle, who is a doctor in a small town a hundred miles away, is already planning to enlist in the Canadian medical corps because he cannot wait to fight against the Germans. We follow the news from Europe and Japan that fall with more than passing interest. Almost all the war news is bad.

Now I am fifty-seven and a journalist/historian. I realize that for a very long time in the earlier part of my life I dated my personal history by means of baseball. That is, I could remember where I was and what was happening in the world and my relation to it by dint of what was happening in the world of baseball: I was in Nashville in 1956 covering civil rights and politics in the year that Don Larsen threw a perfect game. Later, as a foreign correspondent and then as a writer of books, I was able to date exterior political events by remembering what I was writing or where I was stationed. With that, baseball as connecting link to personal history became more ancillary; that is, the great World Series of 1975 happened just after Watergate was over and as the last American troops left Vietnam and as I was writing *The Powers That Be*. At one point the two curves of my life actually intersected: in 1961 *The New York Times* decided to send me, a very young and newly minted reporter on their staff, perhaps the most junior person they had, to the Congo to cover the fighting there, and in the ten days that I stayed in New York City in order to get my vast variety of exotic injections before flying out to Leopoldville, I watched Maris and Mantle regularly on WPIX, and I sensed that something epic was happening in terms of baseball. They were already ahead of Ruth's mark, and the New York papers were beginning to show their records side by side with Ruth's. I remember with great clarity Maris's stroke, so tight and controlled and disciplined. He had Mantle hitting behind him from both sides; he had a lineup filled with good hitters. He was going to get a lot of at bats. He was going to see a lot of good pitches. On a team of mere mortals he might walk a lot, but there was the godlike Mantle batting behind him. Maris was clearly seeing the ball very well, better than he ever did again in his career. I looked at him on the small black-and-white screen in my hotel room, and I thought to myself he might just do it. That short compact swing was perfect for the Stadium. Each home run seemed to be perfectly aimed, sharp right, to right-center, and to have just enough carry. So that year was doubly derivative: there was the beginning of the serious part of my own career, I had always wanted to be a foreign correspondent and a foreign correspondent I had become, and there was still my ability to chart history from baseball.

I went to the Congo, which was torn apart by the political convulsions that came with the gift of instant independence, and became a war correspondent. It was dangerous, sometimes feverish work, one never knew which side was the more hostile, and the one thing we made sure of was not to wear the khakis—the bush shirts and jackets that became the common denominator of war correspondents in most tropical parts of the world, but which in this strange land somehow identified you immediately as an enemy combatant. Instead, we wore our loudest shirts and pants. It was exciting, heady, dangerous stuff, and I was eventually nominated for the Pulitzer Prize for my reporting there (they gave it to Walter Lippmann instead, I would have to wait my turn). I did not, for all of this, forget my larger obligations to monitor baseball as well. I almost never saw *The Times* itself, and if the paper ever arrived in the Congo it was likely to be two or three weeks old. The communications in those days from Leo to my home base in New York were primitive. We filed by telex to Paris, and then our stories were relayed to New York. I had a friend in the Paris bureau and if he did not actually care about baseball, then he at least knew about it, and when my story was done, I would communicate with him on the open telex wire, two men spread across the world, speaking through talking typewriters. I would type out live on the machine: "H...o...w ...a...r...e... M...a...r...i...s ...a...n...d ...M...a...n...t...l...e ...d...o...i...n...g?" He would type back, knowing I would ask, "M...a...r...i...s... a...t... 5...3,

....

...M...a...n...t...l...e ...t...r...a...i...l...i...n...g ...h...i...m, ...t...h...e
...N...e...w ...Y...o...r...k ...s...p...o...r...t...s...w...r...i...t...e...r...s
...s...e...e...m ...t...o ...g...i...v...e ...t...h...e...m ...b...o...t...h
...g...o...o...d ...s...h...o...t...s...."

But let me give you the antecedents of my short sweet history of life through baseball: in 1946 I knew the war was finally over, not just because my father had come
back from overseas after four years away, but because the real baseball players,
DiMaggio, Rizzuto, Keller, and my beloved Henrich for the Yankees and Williams and Pesky and Doerr, were back. In mid-August, to celebrate my brother's
birthday—he turned fourteen that month—my father took us from Winsted, Con-
necticut, to the Stadium. This was a grand day, a day with my father at the Stadium,
in box seats, the Yankees against the Red Sox (the Red Sox had already made a
shambles of the race). Ted Williams hits two home runs that day, one of them off
Tiny Bonham, a shot into the third tier, which is still the hardest hit ball I have ever
seen. Aaron Robinson, the reserve Yankee catcher, hits two for the Yankees. On
the way back to Winsted we stop at a restaurant in White Plains. I think it was Dick
Haymes's Restaurant, named after a popular crooner of the time; the manager, al-
though not the famed Dick Haymes, comes over and questions my brother and me
closely about the game, and we describe it in infinite detail. We are allowed to order anything we want on the menu, which is something we could never do during
the war, when if we ate out we ate at diners and ordered blue-plate specials. I am
warmed by the sense of this as a lyrical day: the war is over, my father is back, he
has treated my brother and me to the perfect day, Ted Williams has hit two home
runs, but the Yankees have won, and we are eating lobster.

And so I can remember other dates this way: 1950 is the year of the Korean War,
but far more importantly my father dies from his second heart attack. For reasons
that I do not understand, my mother and I—my brother was still away at college—
have to go to the hospital to talk to authorities there after he had died. I still remember that trip with my mother after we get the news as the single loneliest moment of
my life and I am devastated. I remember each of the following days with the most
excruciating detail, a series of grown-ups coming up to me, it seemed, and ex-
plaining to me what my obligations were going to be, and how I, now barely sixteen, was going to have to be a man. I was not a man, I was not even close. All sorts
of people, family members and friends, come up to me in the next few days and tell
me how well I am dealing with it. The truth is that I am not dealing with it at all. I
take every memory and in effect freeze it, unable to talk about it with anyone, barely able even to weep. That freeze lasts a long time; it is many years before I can
even talk about it. Instead to the degree that I was able to show emotion, I show it
through baseball. It is the season that the Yankees seem to be coming up short on
pitching, but they reach down and bring up a cocky young pitcher named Whitey

Ford. My thoughts that summer are an odd, badly assorted blend of the real and of fantasy, of the distant and the near: the cocky young Ford pitching as if born only to pitch in the Stadium, the aging DiMaggio increasingly frustrated by the deterioration of his skills, and the unbearable pain of missing my father. In this, the fate of the Yankees seems easier to comprehend than my own daily life: the Yankees manage to hold together and make it into the World Series, their fourth in a row, where they dispose of the Phillies in four rather close games. I do not realize this, but I have done something fairly typical of journalists: confronted with crisis in my own emotional life, I have learned to deal with it by concentrating on exterior events.

And so it goes: I am a college graduate now, working as a reporter in Nashville, Tennessee, and I blend the different memories of 1956. It is the year of Suez. The news that the United States has stopped French and British and Israeli paratroopers from taking control of the Suez Canal seems puzzling; at the same time Soviet troops and tanks crush the Hungarian uprising. This is also, however, the year of the Larsen no-hitter and not surprisingly I have the clearest memory of where I am at that moment. I am a police reporter working for *The Nashville Tennessean*, and that day I have finished my rounds early and have walked back downtown to talk and gossip at Zibart's Book Store, which is run by close friends and which I have come to use as a social club; in the clarity of my mind (which may not be exactly the same as the reality of events) we are watching the games on an old black-and-white television set—the nation is wired by now, and it becomes clear to me about the sixth inning, the way the camera keeps going back to the scoreboard, that the Dodgers have not yet had a hit. There are, as I recall, a number of pointed references about how many batters have come up and how they have been set down. I have a sense from the sixth inning on that it is a no-hitter, and soon I figure out that it may be a perfect game. Four years later, in 1960, it is the year that John Kennedy runs against Richard Nixon and it is also the year the Yankees relief pitching fails and the Pirates come back to win the seventh game. What I remember most about that Series is that for the first time (I am a hopeless American League fan) I do not merely see, but I *comprehend* Roberto Clemente—that is, I get it for the first time, that he is different, special. Before the Series I had heard a good deal about him, but it had been a vision filtered through the prejudice of the time; the word about him for example in the New York newspapers was that the Yankee players did not like Clemente, that they thought he was a hot dog, and I had accepted that at face value since the Yankees were my team. But it became obvious during the Series that he was not a hot dog, that these moves were not an affectation on his part, they were simply and naturally a part of who he was, that he had a gift on the magnitude of Williams and DiMaggio, Mays and Robinson. In retrospect it is my first encounter with cultural differences in the world of sports. There will be many more to follow.

Now my own life begins to take over: the real world is beginning to take precedence over my fantasy world. As I go off to the Congo, I begin to date things differently. I am in Vietnam in '63. I am completely caught up in events there, not merely the events that signify the beginning of a distant, difficult, frustrating war, but even more the ancillary events that reflect that reporters who are pessimistic like me will be the targets of the government. Never have baseball events seemed more removed from reality: the Series is over before it even seems to start. Four games. The Dodger pitching destroys the Yankees. A sweep. I am some twelve thousand miles away, trying to stay alive and fighting for my professional reputation, and I have no time for sweeps in baseball. The next year, I remember equally well, it is 1964, and I am in Mississippi, covering the beginnings of Freedom Summer: those events are transcending, and it is a scary time in America. In the late summer, exhausted, terrified, and terrified in a different way—it is one thing to be terrified in the Congo or Vietnam, it is a very different thing to be terrified on native soil—I return to New York. Vaguely, I sense that the Yankee dynasty is over, that it is crumbling before me, that Mantle after some fourteen years has gotten old, that the farm system can no longer replenish the team, and that the old tried and true power moves, using Kansas City as a minor league team, are finished. What saves them is the arrival from the minors of the young Mel Stottlemyre. Bobby Kennedy is running for the Senate, I have been assigned to him, and I am covering him in upstate New York while trying to pick up on the radio an early Stottlemyre start, hoping he can, as predicted, keep the ball on the ground. He can.

It is like that from then on in my life. In the late summer and early fall of 1967 I am back in Vietnam, melancholy about the huge American presence there, and I sense that it exists at a terrible human price, we are neither winning nor losing, our gallantry permits us to stay but not to make progress. The only thing that cheers me is the stunning personal exhibition that Yaz is making as he leads the Red Sox to the pennant. Every morning, I go over to the Associated Press office along with a few friends, where, because of the time difference, the ticker is clicking off his deeds from that night's game in Boston, and it seems of a piece: Yaz two for four, three RBIs, one sensational game-saving catch. At a moment when I am deeply depressed about the war, and my country, Yaz reminds me that there are things about America I still love and that all of this depression, this terribly sad war, will someday pass.

I ponder these things as I look at Danielle Weil's extraordinary photographs. She brings to something old an eye that is completely fresh and new; where others see what they have always seen, she sees not just the predictable characters and the ordinary scene, that which has always been captured in the past, but she also has a remarkable sense of the lines, of the *geometry* of the game, of angles and proportions. It is a cool eye, original and creative. The angles and the lines of baseball teach, of course: they have their own inviolable truths, the lines of the foul lines in the late innings when the infielders have to protect against extra-base hits. The angles of the corners in the outfield when the outfielders, chasing a ball in the corner, are moving away from the infield and away from their throwing strengths. Seeing her pictures, I think again for a moment of Clemente and I understand why he was so brilliant, so quick, so powerful, so athletic, that he could go against the angles into the right-field corner, away from his strength, but still use his great athletic ability to spin and throw to the plate. He defied not just the opposition, not just the Yankees, he defied geometry.

I am also moved once again as I look at her photos, by the sense of timelessness of baseball. More than any sport I know, it summons the past. In football, photos of another era make that era look dated, the helmets look too dinky, the players look too small; in basketball, the players look too white. But in baseball, it is as if there is a linear path, it is where, in our society, yesterday and today collide: the boy is thinking of the power of the young Kevin Maas; the father, looking at Maas, is seeing the same short compact stroke and thinking of Roger Maris; the son sees the awesome power of Doc Gooden and thinks there has never been a power pitcher like him, the father sees Gooden and thinks of Bob Gibson, and the grandfather sees the same player and thinks of Bob Feller. Time merges in baseball. I am at the Stadium in June 1989, and it is Father's Day, and I am holding my eight-year-old daughter's hand. Just a few days earlier we have watched a game on television and the Mets, unlikely though it seems, have stolen two bases in a row. ''Daddy, is it a good thing or a bad thing to steal a base?'' she asks. This brings me back over forty years to my first visit to the Stadium in 1939: someone is yelling to the pitcher to walk a batter, and I ask my father why the batter is walking, not running, to first. Now we are in the Yankees' broadcast booth, and my daughter watches me as I joke and trade stories with a small older man who is wearing dark glasses. She sees this man who is with her father, and she is told that he is Phil Rizzuto and that he was once a great player; but I am there and I am remembering the rookie shortstop who broke in in 1941, in the year we went to war, and I am remembering that the sportswriters worried about whether he was too small and too green (he was neither, he lasted a long time, he seems to go with the premises), and most of all I remember as I hold her hand now, how my father held my hand then when I was seven, as she is now eight. In baseball, more than in anything I know, today is not merely today, it is yesterday as well.

S PRING T RAINING

With each passing summer it feels as if we're losing more and more of the game—to its lawyers and agents and front-office spokesmen, to its marketers and mascots and promoters. During the regular season, we can hardly afford to visit the ballpark anymore—and when we do, the game itself is overwhelmed by the sales pitch: buy the official batting helmet, buy the home video, visit the advance-ticket window.

In the morning paper, the news accounts are overflowing with this player's contract status and that player's salary, this team's television revenues and that team's payroll. As salaries increase in extravagant fashion, so does the pressure on the players to achieve perfection, so that the athletes grow increasingly truculent, the fans increasingly belligerent.

It is not always so. There remains one major-league baseball season that belongs to the game. For a single month each year, in miniature parks dotting the Western desert and the Southeastern swamp, the big leagues are still real enough to feel unfiltered, close enough to resonate with the simple physical beauty that first lured us long ago. Trees are never far away from spring baseball; artifical turf unheard of; smaller stadiums let more of the sky into a baseball game.

But the intimacy of spring-training games is more than a physical thing. In March, when the stakes aren't high—when one bad outing by a pitcher is insignificant, when five losses in a row are no cause for concern—the tension of the players lessens, too, so that the bond between the men in uniform and the people who come to see them is as strong as it ever gets. In spring, the ballplayer is far less the superstar and far more the casual acquaintance of us all. So that in Yuma a bare-chested retiree can settle into the buttery sun to buy a vendor's beer from a plastic bait bucket and call out to the player in the on-deck circle—and the player will turn and smile back. So that on the west coast of Florida, where a dozen teams train within a few hours' drive of each other, the vacationer will not be surprised to find himself shoulder to shoulder with his home team's shortstop at the local beer-and-chicken-wing joint.

In spring training, the early visitor to the ballpark will see the third baseman hitting fly balls to his kids and the late-afternoon lingerer will be delighted to find that the minor-league player elevated to major-league status for a day will gladly tarry afterward to autograph everything in sight.

In March, even the increasingly adversarial relationship between the game's athletes and its chroniclers is swept away by a salt-scented wind, and the good stories flow: in Lakeland a few years ago, the new Tiger first baseman wanted to talk about the UFO he'd seen during the winter instead of the forty home runs he'd hit the summer before. Then the first baseman went out and swatted a home run, and the writer retired to the third-base seats, baked by the central Florida sun, to watch the game. The story could wait for the evening deadline. In the spring, and only in the spring, baseball is restored to its rightful spot in the daylight.

It's not the only difference between spring and summer baseball; in many ways, the spring game is a different game, and everything about it speaks of the sense of ease that used to define the sport. By the third inning, players are running wind sprints in the outfield. By the sixth inning, the scorecard is so crowded with substitutions that keeping track of the action is a hopeless task, willingly abandoned. And by the eighth, the game is being played by players whose uniforms bear impossibly high numbers—the stars of tomorrow, or, likelier, the failures.

Of course, for those players trying to earn a spot on the big-league roster, spring is white hot with anxiety, and for the serious, frantic fan, the devotee who made his pilgrimage down from the Northeast to see his home team up close, there is no lack of drama: the aging outfielder striking out three times in a row against the other team's second-line starter brings a wince of the heart; to be in the grandstand on the March afternoon when last year's first baseman in Oklahoma City hits for the cycle is to see a star being born. Spring baseball means finding new, ever-younger heroes to watch as they climb through the ranks. Spring baseball is the chance to see them before they become weighed down with all the tedious baggage of self-importance.

And finally, as the weeks of March wear on, a new drama begins to build: the anticipation of the real season to come. Six weeks of sun-sweet breezes, in the end, are more than enough.

Spring training's future holds less and less promise. Fewer and fewer remnants of old Florida remain. The past half-decade has seen lovely old quonset-roofed bandboxes in Tampa and Miami and spindly old wooden parks in Sarasota and Dunedin and Fort Myers abandoned in favor of featureless concrete camps in towns like Port St. Charlotte and Port St. Lucie, communities built by development corporations carving up one of the last virgin states.

The new parks have too much symmetry to them, and too few ragged edges. The rough hand-painted advertisements on the outfield wall of Miami Stadium, the tunnel where you had to duck your head beneath the gray timbers on the first-base side of Sarasota's Payne Park, the steel struts that held up Al Lopez's corrugated sheet-metal roof in Tampa (and the drumming thunder of the summer showers on that archaic canopy)—all these are out of the game now, having given way to the impassable chain fences in the blindingly bright new compounds, with their ''players only'' parking lots attended by security forces packing scowls.

As Florida fills to the brim with an unchecked migration, the stands of the new parks are filled—many of the games even sell out well in advance—less frequently than ever by the gentle, aging congregant at home in the spring game's quirky old homes and more frequently by his unruly, and rude, descendant.

But, inevitably, the spring game will resist the modern, mercenary intrusions. As long as the game itself escapes to the south, it will remain unfettered. As long as the spring game means nothing in the standings, it will still mean everything to the fan.

—— McKechnie Field. Bradenton, Florida. March 1991 ——

—— New York Yankees. Fort Lauderdale Stadium. March 1991 ——

—— New York Yankees. Fort Lauderdale Stadium. April 1990 ——

21 ——

— Baltimore Orioles. Miami Stadium. April 1990 —

Atlanta Braves vs. New York Yankees. Fort Lauderdale Stadium. April 1990

—— Al Lang Stadium. St. Petersburg. March 1991 ——

— Al Lang Stadium. St. Petersburg. March 1991 —

THE STADIUM

In the Bronx, the stadium overwhelms the sky as soon as the subway hurtles out of the tunnel's darkness—huge, numbingly out of scale, overwhelmingly familiar. In Boston, the first glimpse is more subtle: to the fan walking the narrow streets off Kenmore Square, the brick wall on Lansdowne Street suggests nothing more than a warehouse—until the eye strays upward, to the light towers and the net that cradles the home runs. In Cincinnati, city strollers can round any of a number of bends to be greeted, suddenly and delightfully, by the huge white saucer perched on the banks of the Ohio.

Classic city palace or suburban plastic cereal bowl—the effect is always the same: the first time we shoulder up against the buildings that house the game of baseball, we are instantly at home.

The first time, and the thousandth.

Inside, of course, the effect is equally stunning: acres of emerald encased in industrial American steelwork, curves of concrete embracing vast spaces of too-green carpeting—a landscape we find nowhere else in our experience.

At its heart, baseball is an agrarian game; it's the pastime that welds pasture to city. And so the ballpark's appeal doesn't lie solely in its promise that there's a game to be found within its walls, but also in its mission to protect that game and that part of our heritage. The ballpark heralds nothing less than a piece of the past nestled within it.

Its size assures us, too. A building big enough to command whole city blocks is a building to be trusted. Our cities are full of outsized structures, but few hold the intrigue of a ballpark, few command such guttural awe. Few can hold so many memories or pass them so effectively from generation to generation down such a particular path. From the same box seats—say, that odd section next to the right-field foul pole that faces the outfield instead of home plate—the father watched Ted Williams prowl left field at Fenway; the son saw Yastrzemski, and the grandson cheers Greenwell. In the Bronx, the grandfather watched DiMaggio roam the same center field that Mantle roamed for the son—as both were spectators perched in the upper deck and looking down on the same Bronx landscape of brick and water towers that graces the urban horizon beyond Yankee Stadium's center-field wall.

To the purist, the old parks are the most entrancing; the few remaining structures of the dozen built before the First World War are monuments to American history as well as American sport. They fit the grids of the old city streets. They're fashioned from the materials that built the city that surrounds them. They're packed with the juts and shadows and angles of an older America, and they delight with simple aesthetics.

But it would be a mistake to slight even the most monstrous of the modern parks. The multiuse Leviathans—the domes with their humpbacked roofs of polyurethane, the cookie-cutter bowls of the 1960s and 1970s—are full of memories of their own. The nature of a building's soul, after all, isn't dictated by its shape, but by its significance. Rail against the slug-eyed architects of Three Rivers and Riverfront and Veterans, by all means, but there isn't a single one that in our collective memories doesn't dwarf the impersonal post-Bauhaus glass towers of our downtown canyons or our astonishingly forgettable airports.

The game itself can endow even the most cumbersome stadiums with dignity. For years, cavernous Forbes Field was baseball's only shrine in Pittsburgh, its distinction epitomized by Bill Mazeroski's ninth-inning home run in the 1960 World Series clearing the ivy-covered wall in left field as Yogi Berra stood with his back to the plate, watching its flight. But when Willie Stargell and his Pirates won the '79 Series in Three Rivers and their wives hopped up and danced on top of the

—— Tiger Stadium. Detroit. August 1990 ——

home dugout, the new park achieved its own instant and lasting prominence.

When Pete Rose looped his single to left center field in Riverfront Stadium in August of '87 to un-tie Ty Cobb, not only was the ungainliness of the stadium forgotten, the plastic bowl now seemed the most appropriate of settings: a modern arena for a modern record, perfectly equipped to capture the moment when the mantle of "game's greatest hitter" passed from the past to the present. Rose's record-setting hit was a long, high-arching single, its flight played out against a background of thousands of delirious Cincinnati faces—it seemed as if there were millions—filling the curving, distant layers of seats that characterize the modern stadium.

When the Mets and Astros dueled for sixteen innings in the sixth game of the National League playoffs in 1986—the greatest playoff game since the playoffs' inception—no one was heard to slur the awkward, badly aging Astrodome. In fact, the old girl never looked so beautiful. And a few weeks later, in that most memorable of World Series, even Shea Stadium took on a glitter, despite the rock videos barking from the scoreboard and the litter skating across the field. After Mookie Wilson's grounder skipped beneath Bill Buckner's legs, no one came away feeling indifferent about Shea.

This is not to overlook the obvious: that most of the ballpark's appeal can be traced to the wealth of childhood memories it contains, and the special way in which a ballpark's unusual geometry can frame them. If the baseball moments of our lives don't diminish over the years, give some credit to their delightful and singular setting: a diamond traced onto a wedge of green, encased by a horseshoe, or a circle or an oval or an asymmetrical shell bound by the city's grid. It wasn't just the banks of paned windows or the closeness of the seats to the field that made Ebbets Field so memorable; it was the angles of the outfield walls as well—seemingly changing direction every few yards. In Baltimore's new stadium, a paean to all the good of the old, the outfield walls are full of odd angles, on purpose.

And the peculiar pieces of baseball's distinct architecture become players in the game. In Tiger Stadium, the upper deck reaches out and gathers in fly balls to make them home runs; in Fenway, the Green Wall rejects them. In Oakland, the acres of foul territory make every pop fly playable; in Yankee Stadium, the box seats crowd the field and gobble up baseballs. No two parks feature the same overlap of decks and seats and columns and planes, so that each one's crowds are configured in a unique fashion—oddly angled conjunctions of humanity. In fact, the new parks are often at their prettiest when their thousands of seats are unoccupied, just planes of plastic swooping through empty space.

It is true that the old parks had more nooks to make them special. In the bleacher seats of the old Comiskey, half the field was blotted out, but if you were sitting near the open arched windows, you could plainly see the freights chuffing their way south out of the city. In Memorial Stadium, every seat furnished a full view of a small forest of pines and dogwoods just beyond center field. And in Wrigley, of course, even in the lean years, there's always the ivy to celebrate.

Time does little to change the buildings. Man's folly does much more. But nothing ever mars the memory of the first sight of the place. And nothing that happens in the years thereafter, not the foundering of the team's fortunes or the fraying of its neighborhood, can dull that sensation. After the first game of a childhood full of a hundred afternoons at Yankee Stadium, the downtown express train rocked along the elevated tracks and scooped up the last postgame stragglers on the platform of the 161st Street station, and out its windows flashed one last glimpse of a slice of green, the empty outfield, before the cars sank into the tunnel's darkness.

But this was certain: that on the next visit, the next time the train emerged into the light, the building would be there, overwhelming.

And it was. It always was. It still is. The game—and our memories of it—safe within.

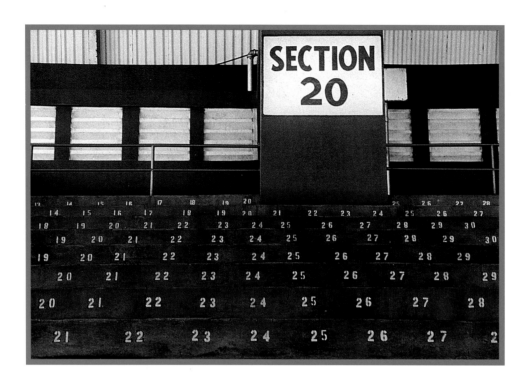

—— Miami Stadium. March 1990 ——

—— Miami Stadium. March 1990 ——

—— Miami Stadium. March 1990 ——

Yankee Stadium. New York City. June 1991

— Memorial Stadium. Baltimore. August 1990 —

—— Yankee Stadium. New York City. July 1990 ——

—— Wrigley Field. Chicago. August 1990 ——

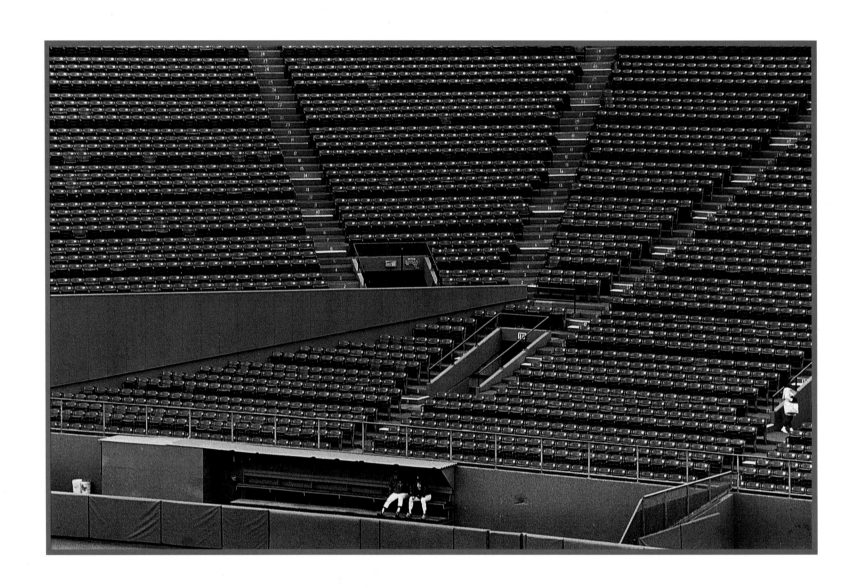

—— Fenway Park. Boston. September 1990 ——

— Fenway Park. Boston. September 1990 —

Comiskey Park. Chicago. August 1990

— Texas Rangers vs. Chicago White Sox. Comiskey Park. August 1990 —

—— Texas Rangers vs. Chicago White Sox. Comiskey Park. August 1990 ——

—— St. Louis Cardinals vs. New York Mets. Shea Stadium. June 1990 ——

—— Shea Stadium. New York City. June 1990 ——

—— Memorial Stadium. Baltimore. August 1990 ——

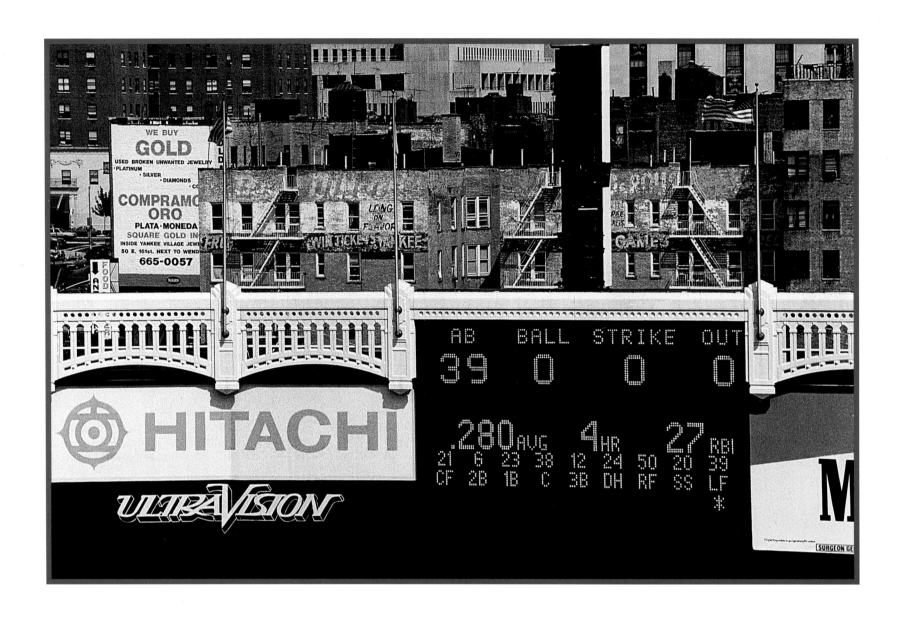

— Yankee Stadium. New York City. July 1990 —

—— Cleveland Indians vs. New York Yankees. Yankee Stadium. September 1983 ——

— P R E G A M E　W A R M — U P S —

The scorecard is clean and unmarked, the pencil stub poised in one hand, the evening's first beer in the other. Out in center field, the scoreboard lists the starting rosters and the out-of-town matchups—with all the games scoreless. The bleacher seats are still empty, except for a band of urchins, gloves in hand, ready to chase the batting-practice home runs.

The curtain has risen—two hours before the game begins.

In other sports, the time before the contest is a necessary but meaningless prelude, unaccompanied by ceremony. But in baseball, the pregame is deliciously personal, and we are privy to it. Baseball is the only show in the land where the time before the game can be as special as the performance itself. For all its informality, it is no less full of ritual: from the first casual lobs of the warm-up tosses on the dugout apron to the autograph session at the box-seat railing. Where else—anywhere—can we get such a backstage invitation? At the theater, the actors are hidden from sight until the play begins. At the symphony, the musicians are allowed only a few minutes of discord before the music begins. In baseball, we are invited to watch the pregame play and to see it become, over the course of a lazy two hours, the perfect choreography that is the game itself.

The truest fan traces his first memory of the game not to something that happened during the game itself, but to his first glimpse of the tableau that welcomed him into it: an impossibly vast sea of grass, the familiar American scent of beer and cooking oil and hot dogs, forever soaked into the walls and girders of the park.

But the sensory delights serve only to embellish the overriding emotion of the early moments: the heady sense of anticipation, of knowing that you've arrived in time to watch and hear and feel the ingredients come together. Most of the great joys in life come accompanied by the time to savor them, don't they? It's truest of all in baseball, where the waiting is sweetened by hints of things to come: a single batter, perhaps, mired in a slump, taking batting practice with the help of a coach who agreed to come to the park four hours early to toss him a few fat fastballs. Or a local kid at the plate, a low-round draft pick in his Legion uniform, getting a tryout, accompanied by his high-school coach—destined, perhaps, for a 750-dollar-a-month contract and a uniform in Gastonia or Appleton or Spartansburg. Or destined to go back home.

Maybe there's an older player running laps around the warning track, red-faced: you can hear him huffing, sense him hoping against hope that the regimen will extend his career a year or two. He's wearing just his undershirt jersey—white torso, long blue sleeves—he's let you catch him dishabille.

The game itself is made up of the strictest rules and rituals and ceremonies. That's what makes the time before a game so spectacular: it's impromptu and human. It's the time when players, like royalty unobserved, can make mistakes, and laugh, and goof, and play a little baseball the way they used to play it before it became so outsized, so bloated with puffery.

When the members of the home team straggle into the dugout and out onto the field and pair off to play catch, it's the same game of catch that brothers always play with brothers and fathers with sons.

The pregame is full of clues that the savvy fan will file away to enhance his enjoyment of the rest of the season. The casual fan might regard the ease with which major leaguers loosen up their arms; the canny fan will take note of the pairings and know who's friends with whom on his team. The canny fan will watch intently the swagger and strut of the rookies and see that some are truly cocky, while others are trying to layer their anxiety beneath a veneer of bluster and bravado.

This is the time, too, for the game's humor to come through. Once it begins, baseball sometimes seems to forget itself and become as deadly serious as a chess game. But from time's beginnings, the baseball player has been the original prankster, the Puck of sport, and the pregame is reserved for his finest—and silliest—jokes. He'll sneak up from behind on a teammate having a game of catch and blind him with a glove, just as his partner—privy to the plan—is about to release a high, hard one. A player with his cap in one hand and his bat in another might sneak up behind a teammate and swing his cap next to the man's ear; the victim hears the swoosh, spins around, sees his teammate holding a bat, and instantly turns the color of parchment, certain he's come within an inch of having his skull dented by a Louisville Slugger.

By now a few hundred kids (teen-agers, parents, school kids in packs) are clotting the railing, and the first of the autographs are signed—though not as many as there used to be. These days, an autograph can be extraordinarily lucrative: a star can pick up ten thousand dollars in a few hours of signing at a card show, so why should he give his signature for free at the park? Because, within the walls of the stadium during the leisurely hours of pregame play, the mercenary tug grows less insistent, the instinct for raw cash dulls. And the kid who's perched next to the dugout when the first player pops his head out, like a farmer testing the wind before the dawn, will likely be rewarded.

The reward need not be so tangible; the early arrival in National League parks, for instance, is treated to the pitchers' batting practice. Rare is the pitcher who doesn't fancy himself a closet Ruth or Aaron, and a batting-practice home run for a pitcher will quickly become the stuff of legend. The side bets are steep, the razzing steeper. American League pitchers, of course, have no call to visit the cage and their batting talents atrophy, one of the signs of the modern game.

There are others, like the warm-up jerseys, usually dark in color, and a jarring note. Like the occasional aluminum fungo bat. Or the stretching exercise—the antithesis of football's full-bore drill-camp calisthenics—all full of laughter, and bad jokes, and creakily aging bodies trying desperately to work out the kinks from last night's collision with the left-field wall. Whatever your favorite player's particular demon, watch him closely as he stretches, and you'll note he hasn't broken a sweat.

When the stretch is done, the players spring across the field, even exuberantly—pitchers running football routes in the outfield as other pitchers lob them passes, and infielders lining up to take ground balls at positions they never get to play in games. A coach will hit long, gloriously slow fly balls with his fungo, and the pitchers will form a fireman's chain to relay the ball back to him. In the outfield, the fielders pair off or gather in threes and fours to talk. Here, there's more delightful anarchy: when a teammate lofts a long fly ball in their direction, as often as not they'll stand and watch it sail over their heads or let it drop in front of them, making no effort to catch it. And while batting practice is going on, two coaches will simultaneously slap ground balls to the infield, even as other players are running the bases—and yet somehow this five-ring circus runs smoothly.

—— Pittsburgh Pirates. Dunedin Stadium. Dunedin, Florida. March 1991 ——

But most of the pregame action takes place behind the batting cage. Satchel Paige called it the social ramble, and in baseball it happens during batting practice, at the cage. Some managers grumpily try to invoke the nonfraternization rules between their teams and the opponent, but they never take. Baseball is a social game. It was the first legitimate American entertainment that blatantly lured the work force away from the workday, and ever since it's been the sport synonymous with goofing off. It's always been acceptable for the American worker to call in sick to go to the ballpark; why shouldn't the players enjoy the same atmosphere? Especially in an age in which the player is often deprived of a social life away from the park? Even the least important player on a roster is no longer anonymous, and in his hotel lobby he'll be mobbed by maniacally persistent ten-year-old memorabilia entrepreneurs. For many players, the park becomes the refuge, and the field before the game their favorite playground.

The batting cage is where players from both teams can mingle and catch up on the news. It has become a fast and furious place of late, because now that most players play on three or four teams in a career, instead of just one, they have three or four times as many friends to ply for gossip and greetings.

The handshakes and hugs of the coaches are the most heartfelt. Watch a four-decade man greet a teammate from 1956. Watch them laugh about the days they hung out in the hotel that was torn down in '64. The casual fan will see a couple of old men in double knits having a chat. The canny fan will notice when they suddenly grow quite serious, and cross their arms over their well-advancing stomachs, and one nods over at a rookie on his roster, and they both look at him closely. The canny fan knows to watch that rookie.

The modern game is doing its best to muck the pregame up. In some cities, mascots dressed in clownish costumes try to command the crowd's attention in the mistaken belief that the game cannot survive unless it hurries itself up, unless it fills in the gaps in baseball's particularly languid pace. Most parks have installed huge television screens to replace the old scoreboards, and teams do not hesitate to fill the screens with cartoons and videos and abrasively jangling anthems of rock and roll. Some teams plant cars on the aprons of the field, offering them in contests; others put out circus props for their mascots to do their shabby things. (All of which can make for unusual signs of the times, such as the sight of a radio reporter and a Montreal Expos player retreating into the cab of a contest's pickup truck to do an interview, to escape the din of the batting-practice music.)

In assuming that our attention span is growing shorter, that we are now looking for screech and unsubtlety in our entertainment, baseball's pooh-bahs are not necessarily wrong, but they should know their fans well enough to realize that most of them come to the park to escape the onslaught of television and buffoonery. They should know that what we've come for are the things that baseball does the way it did them half a century ago: the final pregame watering of the infield, the laying of the chalk lines into the batter's box. They should know that we didn't come to see those chalk lines sullied by the mascot riding over them in his four-wheel all-terrain vehicle seconds before he does a jump off the mound, leaving tire tracks across dirt that had been raked into perfection moments before.

There is a *proper* way for the white lines to be rubbed out: the first batter will erase the back line and stand in the back of the box, trying to get a split-second longer look at the pitcher's fastball. Then the next batter will erase the front line, as he creeps closer to the mound to try to hit the curve before it breaks.

But in the final moments in the pregame, the white line should be perfect. It should beckon.

New York Yankees. Yankee Stadium. July 1990

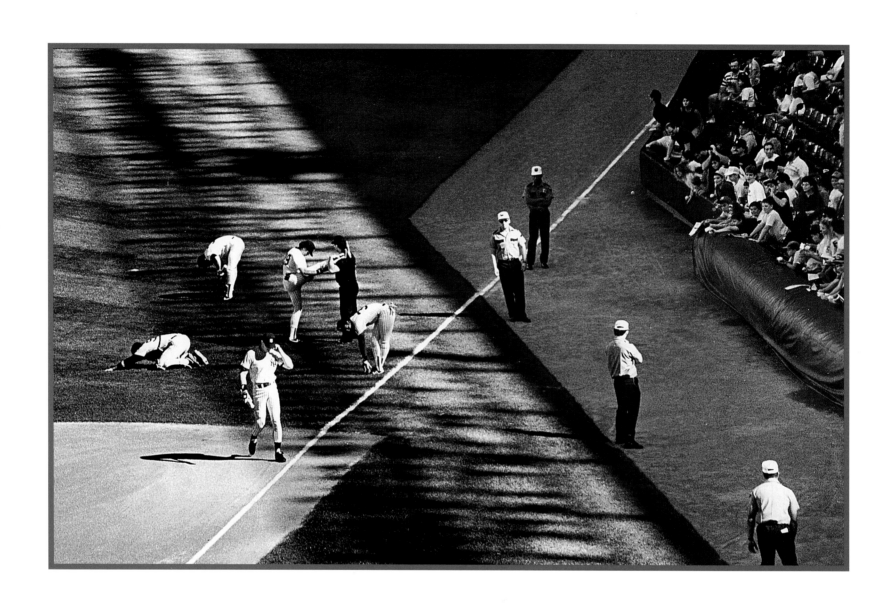

—— New York Yankees. Yankee Stadium. September 1990 ——

—— Atlanta Braves vs. Baltimore Orioles. Miami Stadium. April 1990 ——

—— Texas Rangers vs. Chicago White Sox. Comiskey Park. August 1990 ——

—— Atlanta Braves. Fort Lauderdale Stadium. April 1990 ——

—— St. Louis Cardinals. Wrigley Field. Chicago. August 1990 ——

— Comiskey Park. Chicago. August 1990 —

— Tiger Stadium. Detroit. August 1990 —

—— Wrigley Field. Chicago. August 1990 ——

—— Yankee Stadium. New York City. July 1990 ——

—— Texas Rangers vs. Chicago White Sox. Comiskey Park. August 1990 ——

THE GAME

It begins the way it has always begun—not with a raucous burst of sound, but, fittingly enough for a pastoral pastime, with a sudden hush, the diminishing of the buzz of the crowd as the pitcher goes into his first windup.

In the moments before, the ballpark has been blanketed in sound—fathers instructing their sons, officemates catching up on gossip, friends making bets, all freed from the real-world social restraints by that gentle exhilaration only the confines of a ballpark and the play of a ballgame can supply. But as the pitcher reaches the top of his first windup, the murmur wanes. On the field, the cast is frozen. Umpire, batter, shortstop, the chorus of the visiting team poised in the wings of the dugout—all are posed in a tableau as timeless and expressionless as the figures in a Hopper painting. Infielders lean forward, tensed; outfielders wait, ready to spring to the left or the right, but for the moment spaced exactly where a century of baseball has taught them to stand.

Then the first pitch sails in, the ball thunks into the catcher's glove with an audible thwack, the umpire sings out his call, and the bubble breaks: the crowd's first cheer spills over the stadium, and the game has begun. Exactly as it began yesterday. Exactly as it will begin tomorrow.

For all the seemingly elemental details that have changed over the years—the players, the parks, the shift from day to night, the very grass itself—the game remains quite the same, from the first pitch to the final handshake between pitcher and catcher.

On any given day or night, the outcome can always go either way—the best teams win only 20 games more than they lose, in a season full of 160 of them—but in no sport does it matter less who wins and who loses, not really. Even the most lopsided loss can't diminish the day, because we've come to the park to find not so much a game as an accompaniment, the perfect complement to a special and rare state of mind. We've come for a couple of hours played out in rhythms we never see anywhere else, a pocket where time can pass without urgency, filled with yawning gaps of rest and sudden bursts of animation. We've come not to just see one team win, but to be reassured that nothing in the game itself has lost its power to release us from our daily selves.

The game of baseball is a single act: a man throws a ball, another man tries to hit it. For the most part, the game of baseball is rooted in that cycle: a pitcher and a catcher playing the perfect, endless game of catch. The connoisseur relishes that sense of closure, and all of us can appreciate the rigid tidiness of an exercise in discipline.

But baseball is asymmetrical by nature—its sidelines ever-diverging, its numbers threes and nines—and we delight in seeing perfection break down. When the ball is suddenly flying free in baseball, *anything* might follow. For all of the stunning symmetry of the pitchers' duel, a scoreless game's appeal is an abstract one, a clinical pleasure of the kind that accompanies the virtuoso performance of a piece of music that doesn't touch the heart. The visceral joy of baseball comes when the ball escapes control, takes on a life of its own.

The first hit of the game, a routine base hit—the baseball skipping free for only a few seconds between the moment it leaves the bat and the outfielder scooping it up—brings a thrill that's tangible. (Stand outside a stadium and listen to the swell of the voices that accompanies even the simplest single up the middle, and you'll feel the regret at having missed it.)

If we're lucky, longer hits might follow and bring an excitement that's unbounded, almost illicit: the line drive to the gap flies between the frantic reach of two converging fielders and bounds to the wall, taunting its pursuers. The long fly ball sails over the center fielder's head. The hard ground ball careens down the line, over the base, into the corner. Where a moment before all was in place—the base-

Line drive to third.
—— St. Louis Cardinals vs. New York Mets. Shea Stadium. June 1990 ——

ball cradled in the pitcher's hand, the fielders still, the base runner taking careful, tentative, even fearful little steps toward the next base—now a delightful chaos is astride in the park.

With the home run, of course, the joy *is* unbounded, like the hit itself. The home run doesn't end, not within the boundaries of the field. No other surge of adrenalin can match the sudden flight of the soul when the bat hits the ball with unmistakable authority and promises that it will clear the fence. And if the ball really does carry on and out of the park, the seconds that follow are clear and pure, free of all else. On the field, the outfielder has turned his back to us in resignation, the pitcher paws the mound in frustration and pleads with the catcher for a new ball to rub up.

And still, there's a particular and equally special feel to the loose plays, the error-filled action, when all the careful choreography breaks down. A third baseman will boot a ground ball, an outfielder will watch the ball pop out of his glove, and the unraveling of that single thread can rip wide open the game's whole fabric. With one wild relay, one missed backup, baseball can leap into disarray. The rule book calls mistakes ''errors,'' as if to judge them harshly, but the anticipation of them largely fuels the game.

On a rare occasion, as the innings roll by, apparently uneventful, it suddenly becomes clear that the pitcher has given up no hits, and a special suspense begins to

Two-run homer.
—— Baltimore Orioles vs. New York Yankees. Fort Lauderdale Stadium. March 1991 ——

build. A no-hitter supplies its own kind of theater, a level of suspense unrivaled in sport, and there is no sound like the cheer of a crowd with a no-hitter's final out. The no-hitters are seldom, but regular; their cycle is on a time scale even slower than that of the game itself.

In a game that has no clock, the flow of time is irregular. One at-bat can stretch over ten minutes, between foul balls and pickoff attempts, and another can take a few seconds. There are humps in baseball's time, so that in an hour, nothing at all might happen, and then, in three or four seconds, everything: a bunt single to awaken a dormant offense, a double to score, a wild throw on a ground ball, a three-run home run.

Very quickly, the game breaks down to games within games. When a batter reaches first, the cast of players grows exponentially; the first baseman holds him on, the first-base umpire moves in closer, the right fielder readies to back up the errant pickoff throw. Now the game is between the pitcher and the runner, between the first baseman and the runner, between the catcher and the runner. The edge of anticipation sharpens.

The runner steals, and the whole ballpark tenses. If the call is close, there will be arguing, and the crowd will lean forward in mock bloodlust. No game passes without anger at some point, over a bad call somewhere. But even when the punishment is exile, the stakes are not high. He'll be playing again tomorrow.

Usually we don't have to wait for the umpire's call to know the outcome. If the shortstop makes the tag on the base stealer and then brings up his glove in a nonchalant sweep, we know the man is out; we've seen that stance a thousand times before. When a batter straightens up after taking a called third strike, the resignation in immediately obvious. We've seen that pose.

We've seen them all. Ripken and Ripken turn the double play as smoothly as Trammell and Whitaker did before them, and Kubek and Richardson before them, and Tinkers and Evers before them. They do it as it's always been done; there's no way to improve on it. A strikeout on a fastball will never be an improvement on Koufax. A Mattingly home run, etched against the hulk of the Bronx courthouse out in center field, is only an emulation of one struck by Maris thirty years ago.

More than any player, the pitcher echoes the men who have come before him. The rubbery windup of Marichal, the sidearm sweep of Quisenberry, Dennis Martinez's peculiarly sinewy turn-his-back-on-us windup—all quickly become unforgettable because they offer distinct variations on a motion that has remained more or less the same for a century. There is only one way to throw a baseball overhand.

As there is only one way to play the game itself. Very little changes in the playing of the game. Artificial turf gives us cheap singles and high hops, but the trend is again toward grass. The final groundswell to obliterate the designated hitter is gathering momentum. Even the new stadiums are requiems to the old. So that within a decade or two, the game will have been restored to its original shape.

The odd rhythm of baseball gives us windows, lulls, in which we are allowed to examine its details. In the end, it's the details that stay with us: the routine of Lenny Dykstra's every at-bat, as he pats his helmet, tugs at his pants, and adjusts his wristbands. Graig Nettles' old habit of sweeping his foot through the third-base dirt between pitches. Gaylord Perry's elaborate ritual of tugging at his cap on the mound. So much of the game is spent waiting for the flight of the ball that in one sense baseball is nothing but an assemblage of these moments, frozen into the collective memory of the game. Some are dramatic: the runner diving back to tag the base with his hand and then rising with the badge of scuffed dirt on his uniform chest; the batter ducking away from a head-hunting fastball; the runner trying to break up the double play at second—spikes high—and the second baseman leaping out of the way and still getting the throw off.

Others are less urgent, but no less intriguing: the gathering in of a ground ball, the first baseman's stretch for a low throw. Or even the movement of the whole team itself: nine men arrayed in proportion, then contracting on one play or splaying on another, then always returning, with elastic resilience, to the spots they occupied before. Reassuring. The way they always were, the way they'll always be. At times, in the longest lulls, the game stops commanding our attention entirely. But it never goes away. And even if the action stops, the game doesn't. Just as there is no clock to start, there's no clock to stop.

Much of the time, it's the posture of the fielders that tell us what's going to happen and not the flight of the ball itself. When the fielder turns and runs full speed away from us, we don't need to wait for the ball to fall to know that it will land out of his reach. If he pulls up to trot, we don't have to wait for the cheer from the bleachers to know it will clear the fence.

And when it does, it often puts the game out of reach—in the seventh inning, or the second. And now the crowd noise changes, and attention strays from the game. The chants of the vendors are more audible, the conversation turns to other things. The game dissipates, the conclusion foregone, and the evening's impressions are gathered for pondering on the trip home.

But just as often, the game's outcome is undecided until the end. The winning runner is stranded at second, the tying run comes to the plate. The fielders tense, the batter freezes.

The pitcher begins his final windup, and the stadium falls again into a hush.

And then it ends as it always ends, with handshakes—between the catcher and the winning pitcher, between the man who struck the game-winning hit and the team-mates who have leapt out of the dugout to greet him. If we're truly lucky, we'll watch a home run win a game in the bottom of the ninth and then see the batter round the bases with a jaunt reserved for just this occasion—a style he's affected because he's seen others do it a thousand times before. By the time he stomps on home plate and falls into the glad-hands of his teammates, the pitcher has already slumped into the dugout, and the crowd has long been on its feet, savoring the minutes. Unwilling to see it end. But knowing it will begin anew tomorrow.

—— Follow-through. Texas Rangers vs. Chicago White Sox. Comiskey Park. August 1990 ——

—— Pitcher. California Angels vs. New York Yankees. Yankee Stadium. September 1990 ——

—— The delivery. Cleveland Indians vs. Baltimore Orioles. Memorial Stadium. August 1990 —— ——

—— Brushback. Toronto Blue Jays vs. St. Louis Cardinals. Al Lang Stadium. St. Petersburg. March 1991 ——

—— Ball or strike? Baltimore Orioles vs. New York Yankees. Fort Lauderdale Stadium. March 1991 ——

—— Line drive up the middle. Montreal Expos vs. New York Mets. Shea Stadium. September 1990 ——

—— Fly ball. Kansas City Royals vs. New York Yankees. Yankee Stadium. July 1990 ——

Pop-up. Chicago White Sox vs. New York Yankees. Yankee Stadium. July 1990

——— Pickoff. Chicago White Sox vs. New York Yankees. Yankee Stadium. July 1990 ———

—— Close play at first. Seattle Mariners vs. Boston Red Sox. Fenway Park. September 1990 ——

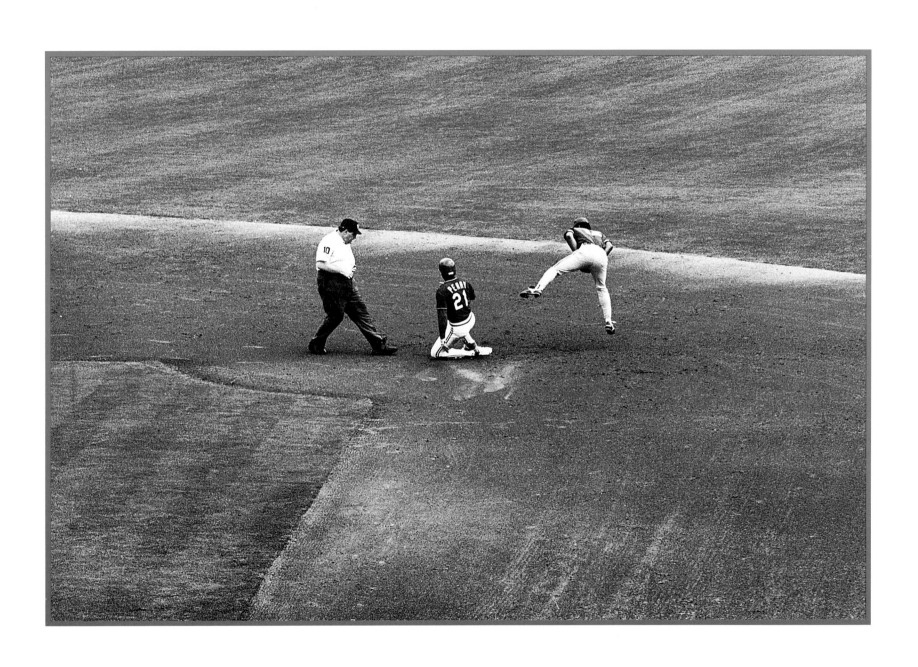

—— Stolen base. Toronto Blue Jays vs. St. Louis Cardinals. Al Lang Stadium. St. Petersburg. March 1991 ——

—— Tough ground ball. Boston Red Sox vs. New York Yankees. Yankee Stadium. September 1990 ——

—— Texas Leaguer. Montreal Expos vs. New York Mets. Shea Stadium. September 1990 ——

—— Strike three. Texas Rangers vs. Chicago White Sox. Comiskey Park. August 1990 ——

—— Long foul ball. Chicago White Sox vs. New York Yankees. Yankee Stadium. July 1990 ——

—— The Green Monster. Seattle Mariners vs. Boston Red Sox. Fenway Park. September 1990 ——

—— Coming home. Texas Rangers vs. Chicago White Sox. Comiskey Park. August 1990 ——

—— Taking the pitch. Cleveland Indians vs. New York Yankees. Yankee Stadium. September 1983 ——

—— Perfect swing. Atlanta Braves vs. New York Yankees. Fort Lauderdale Stadium. April 1990 ——

—— Well hit. Kansas City Royals vs. New York Yankees. Yankee Stadium. July 1990 ——

—— Giving chase. Cleveland Indians vs. New York Yankees. Yankee Stadium. September 1983 ——

—— Home run. Cleveland Indians vs. Baltimore Orioles. Memorial Stadium. August 1990 ——

—— Waiting for the call. Chicago White Sox vs. New York Yankees. Yankee Stadium. July 1990 ——

—— Bullpen. Texas Rangers vs. Chicago White Sox. Comiskey Park. August 1990 ——

—— Late-inning relief. Seattle Mariners vs. Boston Red Sox. Fenway Park. September 1990 ——

—— New pitcher. Kansas City Royals vs. New York Yankees. Yankee Stadium. July 1990 ——

—— On deck. Boston Red Sox vs. New York Yankees. Yankee Stadium. September 1990 ——

—— Sixth inning. Seattle Mariners vs. Boston Red Sox. Fenway Park. September 1990 ——

—— View from the fence. Texas Rangers vs. Chicago White Sox. Comiskey Park. August 1990 ——

Foul pop. Toronto Blue Jays vs. St. Louis Cardinals. Al Lang Stadium. St. Petersburg. March 1991

—— Safe at third. Montreal Expos vs. New York Mets. Shea Stadium. September 1990 ——

—— Play at home. Montreal Expos vs. New York Mets. Shea Stadium. September 1990 ——

—— Crossing the plate. Toronto Blue Jays vs. St. Louis Cardinals. Al Lang Stadium. St. Petersburg. March 1991 ——

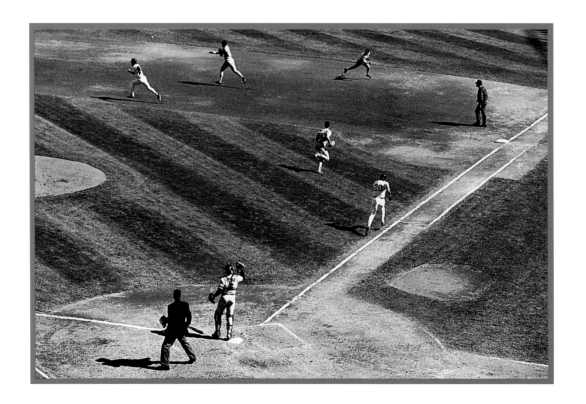

—— Forced play at second. Seattle Mariners vs. Boston Red Sox. Fenway Park. September 1990 ——

—— Fielder's choice. Boston Red Sox vs. New York Yankees. Yankee Stadium. September 1990 ——

—— Awaiting the throw. Montreal Expos vs. New York Mets. Shea Stadium. September 1990 ——

—— Postgame handshake. St. Louis Cardinals vs. Chicago Cubs. Wrigley Field. August 1990 ——

—— Winners on the road. St. Louis Cardinals vs. Chicago Cubs. Wrigley Field. September 1990 ——

THE EQUIPMENT

A young sportswriter leans down to casually pick up a bat during batting practice. Suddenly, a primal bark thunders across the grass. The writer looks up in terror to see the home team's catcher striding toward him, steam issuing from both ears.

"Put it down!" shouts the ballplayer, but the warning isn't necessary. Instantly and instinctively aware of his mistake, the sportswriter drops the bat as if it were a red-hot poker and wonders how he could have ever presumed to pick it up in the first place: why, you'd sooner walk into the Louvre and reach out to trace Monet's brush strokes with your fingerprints than presume to fondle a major-league ballplayer's bat.

And still, it was well worth the effort, for the one, fleeting moment had lasted long enough to feel the enormous heft of the club and the delicate balance as the head tapers to the handle.

As the bat dropped to the grass, the ground gave a little shudder before the catcher swooped in, grabbed his club, and strode back to the batting cage, shaking his head: how could anyone, he was obviously thinking, be so ignorant? It wasn't ignorance, of course. It was irresistible fascination with an instrument of magic, a lure that belongs to all of baseball's paraphernalia. They are more than props for the daily drama; they bear the soul of the game itself: both in fiction—Roy Hobbs' oak-hewn "Wonder Boy" in *The Natural*—and in reality—who can forget that the star of the 1983 season was George Brett's pine-tarred bat?

Season in, season out, the equipment always intrigues us. The rumors are forever flying about which former banjo hitter, now swatting home runs, is corking his bat, or about which aging pitcher, now striking out everyone in sight, is doctoring the ball. We're always salaciously hungry for news of cheating, since it involves the corruption of the game's most stalwart characters. Not the players; they're mortal, and all long lost. No. The balls and the bats. The instruments of the game.

In baseball's equipment, its symbols, we find permanence. The game may mutate, adding a designated hitter, retreating into domed parks, paving itself in plastic grass. But the tools of the game endure, virtually unchanged. The pitcher still fondles a rosin bag; the hitter still rubs his bat handle with the tar rag. The player in the on-deck circle still slips the iron doughnut around the head of his bat. Coaches still bat out fly balls with long-necked fungo bats, as they did half a lifetime ago.

And if we can't trust our favorite players to be there for long—especially as they change uniforms with baffling speed in this age of free agency—we can trust the symbols of the classic teams to stay forever the same: the Yankees' logo, the Cardinals' inimitable two birds perched on opposite ends of a bat, the Tigers' gothic "D."

And if the numbers of the players must, inevitably, change with the passing of the years, the names of the equipment stay the same: Spalding, Rawlings, Hillerich & Bradsby—the same names that we remember from our childhood. This explains some of the fascination: we used them all ourselves, at an age when every sensory impression seared itself into the blank slate of memory. So that when we learn that Tony Gwynn's bat is thirty-three inches long, it is no abstract figure—it's three inches longer than the one we used in eighth grade. When legend tells us that Babe Ruth swung a fifty-two-ounce bat, we can know, in our own muscles' memories, the enormity of that weight: twenty ounces heavier than our own. Impossibly big.

Who knows which multinational corporation owns which team? Who cares? But who doesn't know that each Louisville Slugger is carved by Hillerich & Bradsby? Or that the baseballs are stitched in Haiti?

The baseball is preeminent, of course, in the gallery of the game's artifacts. It bears the name of the game itself. Every moment of the game is spent hitting it, pursuing it, trying to control it, trying to avoid it. And when the game is over, it's the baseballs that become the memorials and testaments to the games themselves.

—— Dunedin Stadium. Dunedin, Florida. March 1991 ——

They're displayed, enshrined, in the living rooms of former players, professional and amateur, across America: the player's first hit; his first home run; his final strikeout.

But not only former players see an icon in the sphere that's simultaneously so soft and so hard; baseballs fill toy chests and rest on twelve-year-olds' bookshelves. The fan who manages to capture a foul ball to take home has captured something ethereal. A moment before, the ball was in play in a major-league game. Now it is ready to be tossed from father to son.

A few years back, when the home runs were clearing the fences with alarming frequency, there was suspicion that the game's ruling minds had jacked up the ball—a rabbit, they called it. How? Maybe the seamstresses in Haiti were sewing them more tightly. And it is true that Bill Veeck, when he owned the distinctly unpowerful White Sox, used to store the baseballs in a cold, dank storeroom to make them harder to hit out of the park.

In this billion-dollar business, with its dozens of television cameras and its instant replays and its multimillion-dollar scoreboards, baseballs are still rubbed down with mud collected from the silty bottom of the Delaware River by one family in New Jersey who have been collecting it for years. They refuse to reveal the location of the source of their silt, lest other miners horn in on their rich vein. They package the mud in old coffee cans. And Major League Baseball remains loyal to

—— Memorial Stadium. Baltimore. August 1990 ——

its product; the game is intractable when it comes to the sanctity of the holy trinity of bat, ball, and glove.

The slightest change in the equipment of the game is viewed with everything from skepticism to outrage. Two years ago, when two outfielders of slight build began to use oversized gloves, it was considered heresy; the two leagues cracked down and forbade their use. The pop-fly machine that showed up in the White Sox' spring camp a few years ago? Never caught on. Charlie Finley proposed a fluorescent baseball for night games; the game shook its head in exasperated dismay. And after years of ascendance, the aluminum bat is now on the outs.

And what of the Japanese firm's computerized pitcher's and catcher's gloves? They knew that the age-old method of getting the catcher's sign to the pitcher—flashing sets of fingers between his legs in a crouch—was imperfect, vulnerable to being stolen by an opposing player on second base or a spy in center field with binoculars. The Japanese gloves, which allowed the catcher to transmit his signals electronically, never caught on; the dignity we afford the game extends to its tools, and the Japanese invention would have cheapened the game, shoving it too far into the realm of high technology, a region from which—at the ballpark, at any rate—we are trying to escape. (It also reinforced the notion that the world needs semaphore.) Baseball is a handmade game, reliant upon the most elemental tools. In the streets of the Dominican Republic, the kids hit stones and fruit pits with bats made of palm fronds. They are no less rich for the absence of computers. Baseball is full of examples of the old world that we have relinquished, from the archaic cut of the uniforms to the scoreboards in Fenway Park and Wrigley Field still operated by hand.

The glove captures the sense of childhood. Who can't remember the soft leather of his first good mitt? Or the childhood debate over the effectiveness of various web designs? Cleats, catcher's masks, these had a fascination of their own, but none as strong as the glove's—the stunning, seamless solidity of the first-baseman's model, the puffy, primal look of the catcher's mitt. Who can ever forget the fragrance? When, bored and idle in right field, an exiled nine-year-old, you buried your face in its pocket, and the perfume—a tanned hide's musk—was almost intoxicating? What little kid didn't store his glove for the winter by rubbing it down with 3-in-1, then planting a hardball in the pocket and binding it up with twine?

When we were young, it was Rawlings versus Spalding. Now the major leaguers use gloves by Mizuno, Wilson, and Easton as well. The bats are not only Louisville Sluggers, but Coopers and Rawlings and Worths—this last a new addition to the catalogue, but its pedigree rings true: according to the legend on each Worth, the bat is crafted in Tullahoma, Tennessee. But for all the newcomers, there is little variety in quality, a testament not so much to the quality of the craftsmanship, but to the ballplayers' adherence to superstition: a hitter on a streak will explain his success in technical terms. He'll never admit what he knows to be true: it's the bat. Yet a player in a slump will quickly discard the unlucky piece of lumber. There are even players, it is said, who will stop using a bat in the middle of a hitting streak, believing that each bat is endowed with a finite number of hits in it. Long lost in the legendary retelling of Bucky Dent's pennant-winning playoff home run in Fenway Park in 1978 was one detail that only the ballplayer can appreciate: at that particular at-bat, Dent had broken his first bat. On a hunch, and beseeching the gods of the game, Mickey Rivers, the center fielder, handed Dent one of his. Dent took it, and swung, and vaulted himself into the corridors of baseball history.

There are new items, of course, that merit less attention—the plastic Gatorade container, the scarlet batting glove, which bears a sponsor's name in such obvious display that it sours our appreciation of it. But not all that is new is bad. Instead of having a helmet turned around on his head, the catcher now wears a batting helmet with its brim sawed off, and a flap of leather hangs down to protect his throat from flying slivers—modifications in armor that you might expect to see in a museum display of the evolution of battlefield attire. To accompany the standard tins of snuff and packets of chewing tobacco, the modern dugout might feature a bucket of bubblegum and hundreds of bags of sunflower seeds, whose shells are now everywhere; they garnish the game from dugout floors to the field itself.

At a Baltimore Orioles "Glove Day" a few years ago, the team gave out plastic gloves, bearing, where the legend of a more traditional manufacturer should have been, a logo with the name of a soft drink. "Genuine rawhide laces," read the inscription; the rest was plastic. The initial dismay at this outrage has been tempered mightily. Not long ago, as my son and I started a game of catch, he showed up with his own George Brett–model leather Wilson and the ball he'd been given by a long-forgotten minor leaguer at a Florida State League game. He also brought the plastic glove, and held it out, and said, "Here's your glove, Dad." And so it is now. It's even managed to mold itself a pocket. The oddest thing of all—it even has a fragrance, and it smells like baseball.

Baseball people who paid attention noticed that Pete Rose was never alone. In the dugout, walking in the runway, or giving an interview on the field, he was always accompanied by his bat. Sitting in the dugout hours before a game, or sitting at his locker after, he was forever hefting it, swinging it, touching it, regarding it. Even when he became the Reds' player-manager, there it was—leaning against the wall of his office, a few feet away, always close enough for Rose to reach out and grab. Finally came the year when Rose was no longer a player, just a manager, and he had no reason to carry his black Mizuno with him. And sitting behind that manager's desk, in his office in Riverfront Stadium, or in Plant City, Florida, he seemed to have lost something special. In the waning days, he seemed to be forever looking for that bat.

—— Al Lang Stadium. St. Petersburg. March 1991 ——

—— Memorial Stadium. Baltimore. August 1990 ——

—— Yankee Stadium. New York City. September 1983 ——

—— Yankee Stadium. New York City. September 1983 ——

—— Comiskey Park. Chicago. August 1990 ——

— Fort Lauderdale Stadium. March 1991 —

Rain delay. Texas Rangers vs. Chicago White Sox. Comiskey Park. August 1990